BECOMING PEARLS

A deep-dive study into God's purpose for your life

by the Wavemakers
Angie Caswell, Christy Payne, and Sherril Weiss

Copyright © 2024 – Wavemakers Life, LLC

All rights to this book are reserved. No permission is given for any part of this book to be reproduced, transmitted in any form or means; electronic or mechanical, stored in a retrieval system, photocopied, recorded, scanned, or otherwise. Any of these actions require the proper written permission of the author.

DISCLAIMER

Although this publication is designed to provide accurate information regarding the subject matter covered, the publisher and the author assume no responsibility for errors, inaccuracies, omissions, or any other inconsistencies herein. This publication is meant as a source of valuable information for the reader, however, it is not meant as a replacement for direct expert assistance. If such a level of assistance is needed, the services of a competent professional should be sought.

Special thanks to our Wavemaker audience, your encouragement and support through this journey. Every live or recorded video, every post, every email, and every conversation are covered in prayer. An extra special thank you to the Wavemakers that joined us in the editing process of this book. You've made this dream possible!

Printed by Kindle Direct Publishing

Printed in the United States of America
First Printing Edition, 2024

ISBN: 9798877337725
Independently published

TABLE OF CONTENTS

THE BEGINNING	1
THE PEARL OF GREAT PRICE	5
PRAYER	12
ENCOURAGEMENT	25
APPRECIATION	35
RENEWAL	44
LOVE	56
SERVICE	72
BECOMING PEARLS	86
APPENDIX: RESOURCES AND TOOLS	95
HOW TO FIND US:	95

THE BEGINNING

Once upon a time, in a town without a stoplight, two country girls lived their lives to the fullest. They shared joy and Jesus with everyone they met. They befriended the lonely and helped others at every opportunity. In their fleeting time on earth (sixteen and eighteen years), they made waves in the lives of others.

Making Waves

On August 7, 2019, after leaving worship service later than usual (due to a baptism), Ella and Aranza Payne went from earthly rejoicing to their heavenly reward. Over 700 people came to their funeral (and most also went to the graveside). These girls didn't just make ripples, they made waves.

Every person we meet is going through something. Ella and Aranza made sure everyone they met felt loved and wanted. In their honor, the intentional Wavemaker Life Ministry began. We want to share it with as many people as possible.

What kind of ripples do you want to make? And why settle for ripples if you can make waves?

Discovering PEARLS

In October 2019, Sherril received a call from a friend in Louisiana, inviting her to speak for a four-day ladies' retreat with the theme of PEARLS. This acronym started all of us on a deeper journey of Bible study in the areas of Prayer, Encouragement, Appreciation, Renewal, Love, and Service. The original date for the event was March 2020. As you are aware, that's also the time that everything in our current society changed. After several postponements, the event occurred a year later in March 2021 but had been shortened to one day. Sherril attempted to squeeze over a year's worth of study into only a few hours.

After that retreat, we began sharing more about PEARLS in our Wavemaker Group on Facebook. Every time we shared, the content increased, not just in quantity but also in quality. We've poured into this topic until it spills out of everything we do.

In 2022, Sherril led a ladies' class during a Home Missions workshop. It was there that we decided to gather this content and create a book for you. The best part of this offering is we are not bound by time constraints so you can dive into this content as deeply as you desire! We have given you the tools to find the **pearl of great price**. The rest is up to you.

Wearing Pearls

This book is designed to be interactive. Write in it, highlight it, make notes, answer the questions, and share with others. As you study, we pray that you also fall in love with the Word as a precious treasure. We aim to present the Truth of God's Word. We've spent hours studying the scriptures to the point of challenging our own beliefs. We **pray** that you will do the same. We will offer **encouragement** along the way. We **appreciate** your willingness to **renew** your faith so that you can **love** and **serve**, fulfilling God's purpose for your life!

Angie, Christy, and Sherril don't hide from those things that are uncomfortable, ugly, or taboo. Instead, we dive into them and speak openly and boldly with God's word as our foundation. Too often Christians keep silent or present a watered-down version of the Gospel in the face of the world's troubles. Sometimes this action is deliberate, avoiding following God's instructions because it is not what we've been taught. Other times, it's due to judging a person's readiness for the Gospel, determining they cannot digest the truth. This pseudo-gospel does a great disservice to people.

The Wavemakers are willing to talk about those things boldly and walk with you through the storms. Throughout this book, you will read our stories and witness our journey to become pearls. We each come from a different background and have a unique perspective. We share those with the intention of making waves in the lives of others. We care about every soul we meet, and you are included in that number!

Each chapter will include questions and Scriptures to study. Consider journaling with these as you go through the book.

Everything in this book has been researched and prayed over extensively. We encourage you to use every tool offered in this book on your own journey to become a ***pearl of great price***.

Unless otherwise noted, scripture references are taken from the English Standard Version of the Bible. Our primary source of information for the Hebrew and Greek word studies is Biblehub.com which contains links to Strong's Concordance, HELPS Word Studies, and Greek and Hebrew Lexicons. This website/app also allows you to see several versions side-by-side for comparison and additional study.

Take a few minutes to think about what you want to gain from this study. Answer this question NOW, then come back and answer again when you complete the study.

THE PEARL OF GREAT PRICE

A pearl forms when an irritant, usually a parasite, finds its way through the shell and into the soft tissue of an oyster or clam. The creature produces nacre which coats the irritant, protecting the creature from damage or infection. The layers of nacre build over time, producing a pearl. It takes months or even years to produce a pearl of significant size. The rounder the pearl, the more torrential the waves surrounding the creature. Best of all, the pearl continues to grow until harvested or expelled from the creature!

We can be pearls. Only healed wounds produce pearls. This process requires diligently covering the irritants - the parasites of sin and the weight of fear - with God's truth and surrounding ourselves with those who will encourage us and keep us afloat. As we learn to surf the waves of life, we become stronger and more resilient. Through the tough parts of life, we become beautiful pearls! We then help others do the same.

Again, the kingdom of heaven is like a merchant in search of fine pearls, who, on finding one pearl of great value, went and sold all that he had and bought it.

Matthew 13:45-46

Pearls are the only gemstone produced inside a living organism. The oysters that produce pearls live in deep waters (as opposed to the ones used for food found in the shallows). Approximately one in ten thousand (1:10,000) oysters produce a pearl in nature.

People who've overcome great challenges often live richer lives. **Overcomers share the best stories and inspire others.** Beauty comes through great pain, resulting in a rare and incredible jewel!

The Merchant

The Wavemakers love words almost as much as we love The Word. When we study the Scriptures, we take the time to define words and discover the meaning in context. What does it mean in the original language? What was the situation at the time? How can we apply it now?

These verses start with the word "again." Jesus is continuing a conversation about the Kingdom with an added illustration. We often need information repeatedly and in different ways to retain what we've been told. The Word of God proves that He loves us enough to communicate patiently with us until we "get it."

In the Greek, "kingdom" means a royal power, a kingship, dominion, or rule, but can also be the physical place, realm, or location of the kingship. This Kingdom was not of earthly dominion, but Heavenly and eternal dominion.

When Jesus first shared this parable, the Jews were anxiously awaiting the Messiah. They believed He would deliver them from Roman oppression and restore the throne of David. Their minds were fixed on earthly comforts rather than eternal rewards. In this passage, the church is the kingdom. We partner with Christ as the merchant to seek pearls.

Jesus gave up the splendor of Heaven to redeem His creation. Just as a jeweler determines the value of precious stones, Jesus determines our value. The loupe (a jeweler's eyepiece) Jesus looks through is not merely a magnifying glass. Jesus sees in us the image of the Creator! Since we are made in God's image, we are worthy of redemption! YOU are a pearl of great price!

Currently, the most expensive natural pearl in existence is valued at one hundred million dollars. In our world, monetary worth is emphasized for almost everything. If you work for a company, you receive compensation. Even if you are self-employed, you are paid for services rendered. When you buy goods or services, a value has been assigned. Even stay-at-home moms are assigned a numerical value by economists, though a mom often counts her compensation in non-monetary terms.

We understand value, though we may differ on what "a great price" is based on personal experience. Most of us would agree that a value of one hundred million dollars is a significant one. Yet Jesus assigned an even greater value to us! We are worth His life! What will you do with such a gift?

The Harvest

Pearls are formed through painful circumstances. A pearl represents a healed wound. Jesus is the Great Physician, the only one capable of healing all our hurts. Even after being added to the church, we will face challenges. Being a Christian is not a safeguard against trials, in fact, the Bible guarantees that we will have suffering in this life. God also uses those circumstance for our good and to reach others.

Christianity is the only religion in which the god comes to the people. God the Creator does what no manufactured god can do. He meets us in the mucky dirty waters, covers us with His love, and offers to make us new and beautiful. People attempt to create gods in human image, often with the worst traits of humankind. God created us in His image and gives us the best of Himself!

When pearls are harvested, they become jewelry or ornaments, their final purpose. When we are harvested, that is the beginning of our purpose. We are not to simply "sit and look pretty" when we've been redeemed. We are called to search for more pearls. Because our lives have been changed, we share that change with others.

Waves create Pearls

Pearls from oysters that live in the depths of saltwater are often rounder and stronger. The waves make the pearl more beautiful! Each pearl is unique, shaped by its environment. In the same way, we are shaped by our experiences.

While pearls can be buffed and shined to appear uniform for jewelry, a closer look reveals distinguishing characteristics including slightly different colors, flaws, or blemishes. As we are shaped by our experiences, we also develop scars – but a scar means the wound underneath has healed! When we look back and see how much we've grown, we begin to see our own journey as a beautiful process of creation.

The same oyster can produce many pearls throughout its lifetime. Older oysters produce finer and better pearls. As we grow, we learn how to adapt to circumstances. We gain pearls of wisdom as we overcome the storms and waves of life.

The next chapters will explore the depths of each letter of PEARLS: Prayer, Encouragement, Appreciation, Renewal, Love, and Service. In each area, we will focus on both the vertical relationship with the Father and the horizontal relationship with others.

Questions:

1. How does the process of pearl formation relate to the challenges and trials we face in life? (Consider Matthew 13:45-46 for further study).

2. In what ways does God coat life's irritants with His truth? (Refer to Ephesians 6:10-18 for deeper insight).

3. How does reflecting on the church being the Kingdom change your perspective of the parable?

4. What do you think about being partnered with Christ as a merchant to seek pearls? (Explore Matthew 6:33 for more understanding).

4. When you consider the value Jesus assigned to you, how does that impact your view of self-worth and purpose? (Reflect on Romans 5:8 for a deeper understanding).

5. How does the analogy of pearls being formed through painful circumstances relate to your personal experiences of growth and transformation? (Look into Romans 8:28 and 1 Peter 4:12-19 for insight).

6. How does the uniqueness of pearls connect to your own uniqueness? (Consider Psalm 139:13-16 for further exploration)

7. How does the metaphor of pearls being harvested and used for a purpose inspire you to actively share your faith and experiences with others? (Refer to Matthew 28:16-20 for guidance)

8. Why is stringing pearls together in fellowship in your own spiritual journey important? (Explore 1 John 1:5-10 for further reflection on the importance of fellowship with other Christians).

9.If you were to fully embrace and trust in every promise of God presented in this book, how do you imagine God transforming your life into something beautiful and meaningful? (2 Corinthians 1:20).

10. What steps are you prepared to take to align your thoughts and actions with God's will and purpose? (Romans 12:2).

PRAYER

When you pray, what does it look and sound like? Do you pray at specific times throughout the day with repetitive prayers? Do you talk to God throughout the day about everything? Do you let Him in to your innermost thoughts and feelings? Do you stick to the basics, or do you go deeper?

Over six hundred specific prayers are recorded in the Bible. In addition, approximately four hundred and fifty specific answers to prayer are recorded. Of these hundreds of prayers, Jesus prayed twenty-five times that are recorded for us and of those, the most significant to us is in John 17. In this prayer, Jesus prays for Himself, the disciples, and all future followers. Jesus knows what is to come and the suffering He must endure to bring salvation to all. He knows what the disciples will face, not only in their initial grief, but also persecution. He knew each of us by name and prayed for our faith and unity as well!

*There is one God and one Mediator who can reconcile God and humanity—
the man Christ Jesus.*

1 Timothy 2:5 (NLT)

Defining Prayer

Prayer is our communication with God, with Jesus as our Advocate and Mediator, and the Spirit as our Intercessor. We have often heard and used these words, but what do they really mean?

An advocate publicly supports and defends while a mediator reconciles differences and settles disputes, creating agreement when there is conflict. As a sinner, we stand in opposition with the Father, choosing our way over His. In this state, we will never be worthy to go before God. Yet He gave us a way to come to Him! Jesus gave His life for our sins. When we accept salvation, repenting and submitting to Him through baptism, we are covered by His blood and forgiven. Jesus negotiates for us so that we come before the Father clothed in righteousness. He stands before the Father and says, "This one is MINE!" (1 John 2:1-2).

An intercessor intervenes on behalf of someone. An intercessor is willing to petition, beg, and plead for someone else. They take the raw emotions and disconnected words of a person and make sense out of the chaos. At times, our prayers may be tears, groans, and even screams of deep pain. "The Spirit himself intercedes for us with groanings too deep for words" and pleads for us according to God's will (Romans 8:26-27).

This communication with God should be continuous. Think of the people in your life that you talk to the most. Angie, Christy, and Sherril have a text message thread that goes back years. Rarely does a day go by without some communication. It is an on-going, open dialog. We can share anything with each other. **That is what God wants us to do with Him!**

In defining prayer, we also must reclaim words the world has distorted. Worldly meditation requires an emptying of the mind, focusing on only the present moment. In Scripture, the word "meditation" is often used in connection with communion with God. In the original Hebrew of the Old Testament, the word used for meditation is "Hagah" which means to moan, growl, or make a noise, as a lioness circling her prey. It is actively thinking over what you've read or recited in a way that demands a physical, audible response. "Yes! Wow! Amen!" In the New Testament, the Greek word "meletaō" is used. This word means to revolve in the mind, ruminate, much like a cow chewing cud. Both illustrations emphasize the importance of spending time in deep communication with God. **Spiritual meditation fills the mind (heart, soul) with the things of God and shifts our focus to what matters most (the eternal).**

When we read our Bible, do we race through it to check off a box, or do we take the time to think about the words? Do we circle them, devour them, chew on them thoroughly? When we talk to God, do we "check in" or do we share everything with him?

The Dare Prayer

Most of us have "routine prayers" for mealtimes or bedtime, especially if we have children we are teaching to pray. We could equate these "check in" prayers with the casual, "How are you?" "I'm fine. How are you?" passing conversations. God desires so much more from us!

If we only pray in this simplicity, our relationship with the Father remains in the shallows. Though God already knows, He wants to hear from us. We really can talk to Him about anything and everything, taking us into a deeper relationship.

What if you changed from the "safe" prayers to a "whatever it takes" prayer life? Prayer ought to be transformative and life changing. A "whatever it takes" prayer molds us into something new. Like the prayers of David in the Psalms, the dare prayer cries out to God, laying out all the emotions, then submits to God's will and resolution. Praying in this way is daunting, even scary at times. As human beings, we like to hold on to our control. This daring surrender gives up control as we submit to the Father.

Our Heavenly Father is all knowing and all powerful, yet He gives us the choice. When we choose submission to His will, we acknowledge and allow for His work to be done in and through us!

When Sherril Prays

We often joke that "when Sherril prays, things happen." Many of these stories are humorous (at least after the fact) but also teach us that unhindered prayers receive unhindered answers.

Perhaps the funniest, but not funny at all prayer, occurred during Sherril's first trimester of pregnancy with Elijah. To understand the context of this prayer, you need to understand that in West Texas we have lots of wind and dirt. Sherril prayed for God to help her get rid of the carpets - her beige, highly trafficked carpet (nine people lived in the house at the time). A simple drop of water would cause a deep brown stain, which spread like someone had dropped the cup they used to wash paint brushes after kindergarten art time. The carpets had to be steam cleaned every three to four months and they only looked clean for a week. This eight-hour job every quarter with only one week of "I feel good walking through my house" led to a constant state of overwhelming exhaustion. Thinking only of floors that looked clean for more than a week without the intense work, in hormonal desperation, Sherril cried out to God, "Help me get rid of this carpet!" Within a week of praying, her prayer was answered, though not as she expected.

At that time, Sherril's sixteen-year-old grandson was staying with them. One Sunday morning, someone flushed the toilet (not just number one) and the toilet kept running until they came home. You may think, "that's not so bad, only an hour or two, right?" That would be true, except that Sherril's husband is the preacher, so they arrive at the church building an hour before Bible class. This happened to be potluck Sunday. From before 8:00 AM until at least 2:30 PM, the toilet ran and ran and ran some more. What started as a beautiful morning of Bible study, worship with great singing, sweet communion, a meal filled with everyone's favorite homemade foods, fellowship, and cleaning up ended in a SQUISH!

As she walked into the house, her foot squished and the smell of sewage reached her pregnant nose. Sherril cried as she rushed toward the sound of running water, turning it off and stopping the toilet. The damage had already been done. The water covered every room of the twenty-two hundred square foot house except two. As they moved twelve five-foot-tall bookcases, a hundred square feet of carpet and pads, paneling, and baseboards to the backyard, Sherril realized what she had prayed just days before. All the books from those bookcases were boxed up and moved into the garage. Fortunately, very little "stuff" was ruined that could not be replaced.

Even though Sherril's "carpet prayer" was answered, her heart remained heavy. Far from grateful, happy, or excited to get rid of the carpet or get new flooring, a new feeling of overwhelm and anxiety took over. The insurance money would not be enough to put the house right and it likely would not be finished before the baby came. Faced with tearing down a load bearing wall, remodeling the bathroom, getting rid of many beloved books, schooling differently for months, and painting all the walls because the paneling was ruined, she was undone because of an answer to her sincere prayer.

Fast forward through all the mess, hard work, money, time, and fretting about the house to a few weeks before the baby was born. Sherril attended several appointments with specialists because Elijah was a sweet, special baby. He was so extraordinary that he had an extra 18th chromosome in every cell of his body which meant they might not get to meet him until heaven. The house was not finished. It was bare bone framework in some areas while half of the family's belongings sat in the garage. Sherril received what she asked for, the carpet was gone, but not at all in a comfortable manner or time frame.

Elijah lived for thirty-two joy-filled days! Sherril spent those days in her bedroom caring for him with all the extras, like oxygen and a feeding tube. Life became a three-hour rotation: one hour of feeding (pumping, tube feeding, cleaning equipment and bottles), dressing and medical protocol (temperature, pulse, oxygen, and replacing the feeding tube after he pushed it out of his nose 8 times every day), and one glorious hour of sleep. Suddenly the home-improvement-show-disaster of the house faded.

Every day was filled with praise for this miracle baby. As Sherril held, snuggled, and prayed for Elijah, she also appreciated every single second. Her contentment ruled the day and her priorities remained straight, for the first time in her life. The Weiss family were sustained by the prayers, love, and food from others who loved them.

Years later, the house still hasn't fully recovered. The bathroom isn't finished. There are no baseboards. There is still a strip behind the front door which remains unpainted. The windows lack framework. There are little holes in the ceiling beside the load bearing beam. However, this temporary dwelling is not the priority. The souls in the home, the people she loves, are the priority (keeping it clean enough to avoid the health department is work enough).

God's timing is always perfect, and He knows exactly what He is doing. Even better, He has a sense of humor. Sherril says, "This was by far the most expensive and hardest answer to prayer I experienced." Now, Sherril looks back in gratitude for her carpet prayer. Through these desperate prayers, God teaches us valuable lessons. So often, we only need to let go and let God.

Provision Prayers

In C.S. Lewis's *The Magician's Nephew*, Aslan, sends Diggory and Polly on a mission. They find themselves hungry and without food when they set up camp for the night. Diggory and Polly discuss their need for food, not grass, with the flying horse that is carrying them through and beyond Narnia. "'Wouldn't he know without being asked?' said Polly. 'I've no doubt he would,' said the Horse (still with his mouth full). 'But I've a sort of an idea he likes to be asked.'"

Our Creator is not much different. Our Father in Heaven knows our needs before we ask (Matthew 6:8). Not only does He know our needs, but His Spirit also guides us and intercedes for us when we don't know how to pray (Romans 8:26-28). **How can we expect something if we don't first ask for it, then seek God's will for our lives?**

Being a military spouse greatly impacts every other part of life. For Angie, the military life created more opportunities to rely on God and trust in His provision. Though prayer,

Bible study, and a church family were important before marrying a soldier, those things became an anchor through deployments, moves, and difficulties of military life.

From Scared to Sacred

When you begin this shift in your prayer life, it may be a little (or a lot) scary. You are not alone in that fear, and you can take courage because our God is faithful and takes care of us. We have a confident expectation that He will keep His promises, bring us through the conflicts and difficulties we face, and give us His resolution.

Our prayer life is relational. Just like a parent wants to hear from their children, God wants to hear from us. This is true whether the child still lives at home, has moved away, struggles to figure out independence, or is thriving with a family of their own. God wants to hear from you – wherever you are in your journey. Until you have a relationship with the Father, your earthly relationships will suffer. Deep relationships require honesty and accountability, an interdependence that builds up each person.

The Bible describes us as sheep. A sheep knows the voice of the Shepherd (John 10:27). In a flock of sheep, one follows another, without thinking about where they are going. The voice we hear is the voice we will follow. If we aren't connecting with the Father through prayer, Bible study, and positive Christian relationships, we are more likely to wander into harm.

Do you ever forget to turn your volume on and miss an important call? Sometimes the volume of the world drowns out the voice of our Shepherd. To hear God clearly, we must be paying attention!

Praying Pearls

When the oyster is infected with a parasite it does not think, "Wouldn't it be nice if I made this into a pearl?" It is fighting for its life, protecting its vital organs. Imagine entering the shell of an oyster and it completely closes, locking you inside. This environment totally covers you in iridescent beauty until you no longer resemble an intruder. The oyster's defense system works continually, covering the intruder until it is no longer a threat.

What if we prayed through our challenges with the same stubborn tenacity? What if we put our energy into daring to pray for change and submitting to that change? God desires to transform us but we must be willing!

Questions:

1. Reflecting on your prayer life, how would you describe your communication with God? Do you find yourself praying at specific times with repetitive prayers, or do you engage in continuous dialogue with God throughout the day? (Consider Matthew 6:5-6 and 1 Thessalonians 5:17 for deeper insight).

2. In what ways does understanding Jesus' prayer in John 17 impact your perspective on prayer and your relationship with God? (Explore John 17:1-26 for further study).

3. How do the roles of Advocate, Mediator, and Intercessor influence your approach to prayer and your understanding of God's grace? (Refer to 1 John 2:1-2 and Romans 8:26-27 for deeper understanding).

4. Think about a "whatever it takes" prayer versus routine prayers. How can you incorporate more daring and transformative prayers into your spiritual life? (Explore examples from the Psalms, such as Psalm 51 and Psalm 139, for inspiration).

5. How does Sherril's "carpet prayer" challenge your perspective on prayer and God's provision? (Reflect on Matthew 7:7-8 and James 5:16 for further insight).

6. How does the shift from fear to trust impact your prayer life and relationship with God? (Consider Psalm 56:3 and Philippians 4:4-7 for deeper reflection).

7. How does the oyster's defense system forming pearls relate to the persistence and transformative power of prayer in our own lives? (Explore James 5:13-18 and Ephesians 6:10-20 focusing on verse 18 for further understanding).

8. In what ways can you cultivate a deeper relationship with God through prayer, Bible study, and positive Christian relationships? How does this relational aspect of prayer contribute to spiritual growth, endurance, and perseverance? (Reflect on John 15:1-11 and Hebrews 10:19-25 for deeper insight).

9. Envisioning the potential outcomes of bolder prayers, how do you imagine your life would be transformed if you prayed with more daring and witnessed God's answers? (Meditate on Mark 11:24 and Psalm 37:4).

10. When you reflect on Paul's final words of advice to the Christians in Thessalonica and your spiritual practices, what actions or attitudes in your life may inadvertently quench the Holy Spirit's work in your life? (read 1 Thessalonians 5:12-19 to get the context).

11. If you were to focus more on eternal matters in your prayers, how would your specific requests or intercessions you bring before God change? (consider the verses in Colossians 3:1-4).

ENCOURAGEMENT

Do you share in both the joys and sorrows of others? Do you have a cheerleader in your life, constantly encouraging you? Biblical encouragement involves "coming along side" to comfort and build up others. What does that look like for us?

Encouragement begins with our vertical relationship with God, receiving encouragement from Him to share it with others. It involves admonishing, teaching, correcting, and lifting one another.

In Acts 4, we are introduced to Barnabas, a nickname given to Joseph of Cyprus meaning "son of encouragement." Barnabus supported himself on his missionary journeys, stood up for Paul among the believers, and mentored his younger cousin, John Mark. While we don't know as much about him as some of the other early church leaders, being known for encouragement is high praise.

Therefore encourage one another and build each other up, just as in fact you are doing.

1 Thessalonians 5:11 (NIV)

Defining Encouragement

Encouragement speaks the truth with kindness. It involves being honest in loving, gentle ways. This occurs vertically, in our relationship with God and trusting His purpose in our lives, and horizontally, in our relationships with others as we connect with others.

The Greek word for encouragement is parakaleó. As is often the case, our English translation and connotations do not clearly emphasize the intention of the original language. The word used here is a calling to come alongside another, a summons or invitation, begging someone to act, and even offering and receiving comfort. Even more significant, perhaps, this was a recognized legal term. Parakaleó is the offering of evidence that will stand up in God's court.

Additionally, the Greek word used for "build" in this verse, oikodoméō, means to properly build a house or to edify. In other words, helping a person or thing to stand firm! One of the best examples of this in scripture is found in Exodus 17:8-13, when Aaron and Hur hold up the arms of Moses so Israel wins the battle.

When encouragement begins in our relationship with God, it allows us to produce more fruits of the Spirit and fosters deeper connections with others. In this context, encouragement (comfort) does not imply the absence of pain, any more than Godly peace suggests the absence of conflict. Instead, comfort signifies having someone walking beside us, providing strength drawn from God. As God comforts and encourages us, we, in turn, become equipped to extend the same to others. True courage emerges when we actively seek God's will.

Encouragement as a Superpower

Biblical encouragement is a powerful force. The Bible wisely states that "two are better than one" (Ecclesiastes 4:9-12). Moses passes the mantle of spiritual leadership on to Joshua in full confidence because he first received it from the Lord. Joshua, in his leadership journey, is commanded to be strong and courageous, with the assurance that God is with him wherever he goes (Joshua 1:9). Later, Elijah prepares Elisha in a similar manner. Even in the New Testament, we see this type of encouragement in the relationship between Paul and Timothy.

Encouragement shows understanding and empathy without diminishing someone's experience. Saying, "I know exactly how you feel" is often unhelpful and untrue, failing to validate others' unique experiences. Expressing readiness to support, without burdening them with decisions, builds trust and security. Simple acts of kindness and practical help offer nonintrusive encouragement.

Encouragement is a spiritual gift. While it may come naturally to some, others must work at it. When reaching out to someone struggling, avoid the generic "How are you?" and instead say, "I've been thinking about you; how can I pray for you today?" This opens a more meaningful avenue for conversation. Other times, encouragement involves removing those obstacles of decision making and providing for a specific need. Some possibilities include taking a meal without being asked, offering to clean the house, or a gift card to help with financial burdens. Personal encounters highlight the power of encouragement. The acts of showing up, being present, and offering practical help highlight the power of encouragement. Sacrificial actions taken for another's well-being often speak louder than any words we can offer.

A Mindset of Encouragement

Seeking encouragement in God and finding a church community make a significant difference. The people we surround ourselves with play a pivotal role in both receiving and giving encouragement. In the vast ocean of life, we often may feel lost. The world around us is filled with political, economic, and societal challenges that create fear and unrest. These feelings impact our mindset and relationships.

Did you know that it takes 40 positive reviews and instances of good customer service to counteract a single negative one? Negative encounters can significantly impact one's perspective on a situation, place, or event. Everyone is a salesperson. Regardless of your life's endeavors, you're essentially "selling" yourself – not in a negative sense, but in the context of whether others want to be part of your life beyond a fleeting conversation. What type of customer service do you offer? Do you convey genuine care and compassion, listening to the opinions and emotions of others? Customer service transcends merely selling a product; it's about building relationships.

Consider Jesus in the wilderness (Matthew 4:1-11). The enemy tempted Him with the offer of all the people of the world if He would only bow down. The temptation to avoid the cross, pain, and death was intense. Jesus resisted, choosing to follow the mind and plan of God. What if we only focused on the truth of God's word, rejecting thoughts of failure or unworthiness? The transformation would be astounding! Not only would we see the change in our life, but we would witness the ripples in the lives of those around us.

Identity is not found in material possessions, status, or external opinions. **Our identity is rooted in being children of God, created for good works that He planned long before our birth.** Despite our failures, God has more for us. When we surrender to His encouragement and exhortation, He calls us overcomers.

Encouragement through Grief

Grief alters brain function. In fact, the actual chemistry of the brain changes during times of grief. The brain demands a different response to continue to keep all systems working.

As Wavemakers, we come alongside those in pain, offering support and encouragement. We aim to be a source of comfort, exhortation, and joy, helping individuals recognize their value in the eyes of God. Our own experiences allow us to empathize and provide genuine support, breaking the cycle of hurt and despair.

Sherril recalls a moment in an emergency room after losing a baby, feeling devastated and weak, when the words from the book of James played in her mind. "Consider it pure joy when you suffer various trials" (James 1:2-4). She struggled to understand the joy in that trial, but with time, realized greater joy and blessings. Later, when her son Elijah received a challenging diagnosis, she didn't foresee the positive impact his story would have on others. His journey became a source of encouragement, faith, and healing for those facing similar struggles. Through her grief, she became uniquely equipped to comfort others.

When Christy's daughters were in the accident that forever changed our lives, we surrounded her with comfort. We also had others supporting us. Our community provided for every need!

Not long after the accident, one of our friends and her son met Angie and her kids for a playdate. During the conversation, the friend talked about the devotional she and her son had recently read about Aaron and Hur holding up the arms of Moses during the battle (Exodus 17:12-14). If his hands were raised, Israel's army prevailed. As Moses grew tired and his arms fell, the army suffered losses. When Aaron and Hur came alongside Moses and held his arms, Israel conquered the enemy. When asked for a practical application, our friend told her son that Sherril and Angie were supporting Christy. She went a step farther, telling him how our community was holding all of us up so that we could stand and prevail.

In our journey, encouragement is essential. It's not about boasting in our own strength but acknowledging the power of the Spirit of God working through us. The lies we believe about ourselves, our worth, and our capabilities are silenced by embracing the truth of God's love.

Consider Joseph whose brother's despised him, threw him in a pit, and sold him into slavery. Years later, when the brothers meet again, Joseph forgives them saying, "You intended to harm me, but God intended it all for good. He brought me to this position so I could save the lives of many people" (Genesis 50:20). Life's trials may seem unbearable, but holding onto faith in God's plan can lead to unexpected outcomes. Joseph trusted God and fulfilled a purpose greater than he could have imagined.

Understanding our value in God's eyes transforms how we perceive ourselves. Encouragement is not just about feeling loved by others but about choosing to receive and give the love that stems from our connection to the Father. Together, we can lift each other out of the pit, hold each other's hands and become instruments of God's love and encouragement.

Pearls of Encouragement

Encouragement is also connected to the concept of courage. While encouragement means to strengthen, courage is the very essence of strength. Where you draw your strength influences how you strengthen others. Your ability to encourage ties directly to speaking kind, truthful words. It involves being honest in a loving, gentle manner.

Encouragement, rooted in God, allows us to produce more of the Fruits of the Spirit, fostering deeper connections with others.

Hebrews 10:23-24 offers a call to action. "Hold fast" to your confession of hope. Believe that God keeps His promises. Consider how to stir one another up and get excited about love and good works. You were created for good works that He created beforehand just for you (Ephesians 2:10)! The Hebrew writer continues the thought in verse 25, "Let us not neglect meeting together, as some are in the habit of doing. Instead, let's come together, encouraging one another even more as we see the day drawing nearer." Often this verse is used to emphasize church attendance. Some versions say, "the Day," as in, the second coming of Christ. Other scholars believe the author is warning his original audience of the coming destruction in Jerusalem, which brought greater tribulation to both Jews and Christians than any other event in history at that point in time. Whatever the case, encouragement is a requirement in the body of Christ.

As we see days of trial, let us encourage one another, let us stir one another up, get excited about love and good works. We are called to be a conduit of encouragement, exhortation, joy, gladness, consoling, and comforting to all God sets in our path!

Questions:

1. How do you perceive biblical encouragement, especially in terms of coming alongside others in their joys and sorrows? (Read 1 Thessalonians 5:11 for further study).

2. How does the Greek word "parakaleó" deepen your understanding of what it means to offer comfort and support to others and where do you typically seek encouragement when facing challenges or difficulties? (Read Hebrews 10:24-25 to gain more understanding).

3. Do you have someone in your life whom you consider a "Barnabas cheerleader," constantly uplifting and supporting you in your journey of faith? (Reflect on Acts 4:32-37).

4. How does encouragement or comfort from God enable us to extend that encouragement to others? (Read 2 Corinthians 1:3-7 for deeper thought).

5. How can you incorporate speaking truth with kindness into your relationships, both vertically with God and horizontally with others? (Ephesians 4:14-16 can help us focus on the purpose).

6. In times of grief and trials, how can biblical encouragement serve as a source of strength and hope? (Read Psalm 23, Revelation 21:4, Psalm 147:1-11, 1 Thessalonians 4:13-18 to reflect on our God's comfort, encouragement, and hope).

7. How have you experienced Biblical encouragement in your life or the lives of others? What difference did this kind of encouragement make? (Read Ecclesiastes 4:9-12 and consider the meaning)

APPRECIATION

Did you know, the simple act of expressing gratitude creates a positive change within your brain? One UCLA study revealed that practicing gratitude for only fifteen minutes a day, five days a week over the course of six weeks enhances mental wellness. Not only that, but this practice may also even create a lasting change in perspective!

Gratitude activates the areas of your brain responsible for feelings of happiness. An attitude of gratitude is God's anti-depressant, built into the chemistry and neurobiology of His creation! (Note: this is not discounting clinical diagnoses or the validity of medical intervention when necessary).

The Power that made the body, heals the body. When we express appreciation to the Father for all He has done, is doing, and will do, our brains create pathways for health and success. After we thank the Creator, we can then share appreciation with others. This fosters deep connection as we build relationships with each other.

Give thanks to the LORD, for he is good; his love endures forever.

1 Chronicles 16:34

Defining Appreciation

Appreciation is the recognition of good qualities. Another definition for appreciation involves a written assessment of value. Appreciation is not only an acknowledgment and recognition of worth, but also worth itself!

In this chapter, and in many of our materials, we use gratitude and appreciation interchangeably. The word gratitude comes from the Latin word gratis, grace or favor. In Spanish, gratis means "free." It should not come as a surprise then that gratitude eases feelings of discontent or stress!

Scripture tells us that thanksgiving is the antidote to worry and anxiety. In Philippians 4:6-7, Paul writes, "Do not be anxious about anything, but in everything by prayer and supplication with thanksgiving, let your request be made known to God. And the peace of God, which surpasses all understanding, will guard your hearts and your minds in Christ Jesus." **The prescription for worry is to count your blessings.**

Giving thanks despite our circumstances is necessary to live for God's will. In 1 Thessalonians 5:15-18, Paul again writes, "See that no one repays anyone evil for evil, but always seek to do good to one another and to everyone. Rejoice always, pray without ceasing, give thanks in all circumstances, for this is the will of God in Christ Jesus for you." God wants us to always be thankful. When you actively express appreciation, joy follows. When you are walking in joy, you have freedom from worry and anxiety.

More than a Holiday

As Americans, we dedicate one day each year to giving thanks. For some, Thanksgiving is so much more than a day off school and work. In Angie's family, the Thanksgiving holiday has always been a time for family to come together. However, these gatherings often included "outsiders." Until 2018, her grandparents hosted Thanksgiving in their home. They richly exhibited God's love and Christ's forgiveness, welcoming everyone, whether the person deserved it or not. After they moved to a retirement community, Angie's aunt took over hostess duties. Despite having a smaller gathering space, everyone was still welcome. Since the passing of Angie's Grandmama in 2021 and Granddaddy in 2022, family gatherings have changed, but one lesson that continues is that everyone is welcome, any time they can come.

As military families, both the Caswells and Weisses learned to create new traditions, especially when living overseas. Both families held an "everyone is welcome" mindset. Sometimes they gave this grace, and other times, they received it. In every case, they took comfort in the opportunity to express gratitude.

An attitude of gratitude goes beyond one day a year or the holiday season. In general, people tend to be kinder and more generous during the time between Thanksgiving and Christmas. As Christians, that needs to be our consistent method of operation. Every day, you can thank someone. Thank your waiter or the car hop. Thank the person at the bank, post office, or grocery store. These people rarely receive a thank you. Thank your children, your husband,

and your friends. You can even thank people you pass on the street. When you express gratitude, you improve two lives!

More than a Feeling

Throughout the Psalms, we see the writer crying out to the Lord followed by praise and thanksgiving. Even during a battle or anguish over loss or devastating grief, David and the other psalmists thanked God. They said, "You know, this is a really hard thing. The enemies are all around me, but thanks be to God for the victory. Praise God that He's given us all that we need." They were even praising Him while in captivity. They thanked Him while they were being captured because they knew that was not the end. They trusted in the Promise. Colossians 2:6-7 says, "Therefore, as you received Christ Jesus the Lord, so walk in Him, rooted and built up in Him and established in the faith, just as you were taught, abounding in thanksgiving." Right after this verse. Paul warns the church in Colossae to actively watch out for false teachers. Thanksgiving keeps us rooted in truth. Appreciation determines where your thoughts and actions lead. **Walking in gratitude keeps you focused throughout your walk of faith.**

Psalm 136 begins with "Give thanks to the Lord, for He is good; His love endures forever," then continues to tell the story of Israel, punctuated with "His love endures forever" after each line. What better reason is there to have gratitude than because His love endures forever? If that's not reason enough, consider what happens in your body when you express appreciation. Gratitude is associated with higher levels of good cholesterol, lower levels of bad cholesterol, and lower systolic and diastolic blood pressure both at rest and in the face of stress. It has also been linked with higher levels of heart rate variability, a marker of cardiac coherence or a state of harmony in the nervous system and a heart rate that is equated with less stress and greater mental clarity. Gratitude also lowers levels of creatinine, an indicator of the kidneys' ability to filter waste from the bloodstream, and lowers C-reactive protein, a marker for cardiac inflammation and heart disease.

If you are a Veggie Tales fan, you might recall Junior Asparagus saying, "A thankful heart is a happy heart" in the Madam Blueberry episode. As you read above, science eventually catches up to the Truth of God. For both your physical and spiritual heart, a thankful heart is happy and healthy!

Conquering Trauma

The word used for "heart" in scripture means "the center of being," not the organ that pumps blood throughout the body. This heart houses our character, desires, and intentions. Just as the physical heart transports nutrients and oxygen, our spiritual heart transports emotions. When you have an emotional or spiritual experience, it shows up physically in your body. Likewise, when someone experiences a traumatic brain injury, it affects their body, emotions, and spirit. We often attempt to fix one part without looking at the whole picture, tackling one problem at a time. For example, we might attend anger management classes to help with our temper but fail to consider how that anger connects to other parts of life. This is not how healing happens.

Trauma, illness, and stress impact all other parts of our health: mind, body, and soul. Robert Emmons, Ph.D., a professor of psychology at UC Davis, has studied the effects of gratitude on physical and mental health. His findings show that the practice of gratitude has dramatic and lasting effects on a person's life. It lowers blood pressure, improves immune function, and improves sleep quality. Gratitude reduces the overall lifetime risk for depression, anxiety, and substance abuse disorders and is a key resiliency factor in the prevention of suicide. Practicing gratitude regularly blocks toxic emotions such as envy, resentment, regret, and depression, which all destroy our happiness. Emmons goes on to say that it's impossible to feel envious and grateful at the same time. In other words, when we are thankful, we have peace, just as we read in Philippians 4:6-7. "Do not be anxious about anything, but in every situation, by prayer and petition, with thanksgiving, present your requests to God. And the peace of God, which transcends all understanding, will guard your hearts and your minds in Christ Jesus."

Brain scans show increased activity in frontal cortex when a person both gives and receives appreciation. This area of the brain is associated with understanding social cues, empathy, and feelings of relief. This area also connects to the systems that regulate emotion and the process of stress relief.

When something comes up that Angie's kids want to pray about, they start with, "Dear God, thank you for this day." Even when the subject of the prayer is devastating news, they still say, "Thank you for this day. Thank you for our many blessings. Thank you for (insert situation or person)." They have done this from the time they learned to pray. Without any medical training, Angie's children figured out that gratitude makes you feel better! Perhaps they've unlocked the key to prayer.

Pearls of Appreciation

William A. Ward said, "God gave you a gift of 86,400 seconds today. Have you used one to say thank you?" God's word says, "Whatever you ask for, do it with thanksgiving." Like Daniel, we should pray as though expecting an answer. In Daniel 10:12 God's messenger tells Daniel, "I already had an answer for you before you opened your mouth." **God wants to answer us; He wants us to be grateful for that answer and start with those everyday blessings.** Start simply: Thank you, God, for the food you put on my table, a comfortable home, freedom to worship, and salvation. From there, you can get specific and go deeper. You will see how each blessing builds your appreciation so that it runs over into your interactions with others.

Questions:

1. How do you actively practice gratitude and appreciation in your daily routine - even amid challenges or difficulties? (Meditate on Psalm 116 and 1 Thessalonians 5:12-19).

2. How would incorporating a daily practice of gratitude impact your overall perspective and well-being? (study the connection between being anxious and gratitude in Philippians 4:4-7 and the effect on both the heart and the mind).

3. How do you define appreciation in your life? Is it merely acknowledging good qualities, or does it extend to a deeper assessment of value and worth? (reflect on Psalms 136 and John 22:14-2).

4. How can you develop a consistent attitude of gratitude in your daily interactions and relationships? (Reflect on the Colossians 2:6-7 as a daily continual practice).

5. When considering the physical and mental health benefits of gratitude, how will incorporating thanksgiving into your prayers and daily life contribute to your overall well-being? (pray Psalm 103 and memorize Philippians 4:6-7 and trust the Lord to show you).

RENEWAL

The original word we were given for the R in PEARLS was "reach," as in reaching up toward God and out toward others. As we developed our material, two other words surfaced: Renewal and Revival.

The first presentation of the material included a trip to Louisiana, lost power point slides, and a broken clock. When the three of us shared this topic in one of our virtual retreats, we titled it "Another in the Fire." We poured our grief and loss into the letter R.

The video livestreamed on August 12, 2021, two weeks after Angie's Grandmama died, two years after the accident, and eight years after the short life of Sherril's Elijah. We took each stage of grief and presented our audience with a message of hope, even in sorrow, tragedy, and uncertainty.

Therefore, we do not lose heart. Though our outer self is wasting away, yet our inner self is being renewed day by day.

2 Corinthians 4:16 BSB

Defining Renewal

Renewal simply means, "to make new." The Greek word, anakainoó, takes that a step higher. According to HELPS word studies, this word means "to renew by moving from one stage to a higher (more developed) one; make qualitatively new." This word only occurs in 2 Corinthians 4:16 and Colossians 3:10 and never in a secular context. In both instances, it refers to God continuously transforming the believer.

Before you read further in this book, read Daniel chapter three. Remember how King Nebuchadnezzar built a golden image of himself, 90 feet high and nine feet wide. Recall how Shadrach, Meshach, and Abednego refused to bow to the idol. Consider their response to the king in verses 16-18, "O Nebuchadnezzar, we have no need to answer you in this matter. If this be so, our God whom we serve is able to deliver us from the burning fiery furnace, and he will deliver us out of your hand, O king. But if not, be it known to you, O king, that we will not serve your gods or worship the golden image that you have set up."

Their boldness infuriates the king, and he instructs that the furnace be heated seven times hotter. The men who took Shadrach, Meshach, and Abednego to the fire were instantly killed by the flame. Then something happens that stops Nebuchadnezzar in his tracks. "I see four men unbound, walking in the midst of the fire, and they are not hurt; and the appearance of the fourth is like a son of the gods." (verse 25). He goes to the furnace and calls them out, while also remaining unscathed. The men walked out unharmed. Their clothes and hair were not singed. There wasn't even a smell of smoke on them! There was another in the fire!

Maybe you aren't sure what this event has to do with renewal or revival. Until you are refined by the fire, you cannot be made new. When working with precious metals, like gold or silver, the smith first heats the metal to the melting point. They scrape any impurities from the liquid, let it set, then heat it again. They repeat this process until they see their own reflection in the precious metal.

In 2018, Hillsong United introduced the song "Another in the Fire." This song takes the event of Shadrach, Meshach, and Abednego and the fiery furnace to illustrate that God is with us in all things, working through every circumstance, to bring us joy and peace. The final chorus says, "There'll be another in the fire standing next to me. There'll be another in the waters holding back the seas. And should I ever need reminding how good You've been to me; I'll count the joy come every battle 'cause I know that's where You'll be!" The lyrics express the profound truth that in our fiery trials, there is another with us, standing next to us, holding back the seas. Even when we can't see through the darkness, the darkness bows to His light.

All of us have been touched in some way by grief, tragedy, disappointment, struggle, pain. If you haven't yet, you will. Whether you've already been through a fiery trial, you're currently in one, or the trial is yet to come, we are promised suffering (read the book of Job, or Romans 5:3–5; 1 Peter 5:10; James 1:2–4; James 1:2; 1 Corinthians

4:8–10; 1 Peter 1:6–17). Whatever your experience is, you are not alone. We all face suffering, yet we are promised that God works all things together for our good, according to His purpose (Romans 8:28). As we face the fire in our lives, we can trust God. He's there, in the fire with us and He already knows the outcome. We can count it all joy because God's already in and through the flames.

A Fourth in the Car

In the first hours following the accident, we held our breath while praying. We waited anxiously for news, while also relieved for every moment without it. When the news reported the accident, every article reported four people were in the car. Angie fielded many calls from people asking who else was in the car, including a panicked message from Sherril's oldest daughter. After confirming there was not an additional passenger besides the three Payne sisters, we filed the information away as a journalism error. That is, until the daylight hours showed the extensive damage to the vehicle, specifically where Sarah had been seated. There was a Fourth in the car.

The accident forever changed our lives, immeasurably. When we focus on the Fourth, we find comfort and renewal. God is with you in the fire or the raging storms. Indeed, there was a Fourth in the car, that night with Christy's girls and He held us all through our grief. There was a Fourth when you battled cancer, a Fourth when you went through a divorce, a Fourth when you were abused and neglected. God is our Fourth, no matter what we go through. He's always there, whether we see a physical Fourth in the fire or not. He is always there. Acknowledge

Him and give Him the glory. Praise Him for saving us in the storm, for being our steadfast anchor. **When we allow Him to be the Fourth in the fire with us, He will use the waves of the storm for good.** It's an amazing comfort to us to know that we are never alone in the storm. God knows what we can do better than we do. He sees the whole story and has a plan and purpose, even in tragic events. God knew the legacy of Ella and Aranza could reach the ends of the earth. He was in the car, as He continues to be with us. He is with Sarah and knows she can do remarkable things, even through the pain.

Presence and Promises

Some people we meet have a presence that seems larger than life itself. They are a force to be reckoned with and command a room with their presence. Angie's Grandmama, Rose Marie Rogers (but everyone called her Grandmama), was just such a person. When she married, two days before her eighteenth birthday, she told her husband that she wanted to have four children by her twenty-fifth birthday. She met this goal, and many others.

She taught Sunday school, led Bible studies, and managed her home. She was an Avon lady and a bookkeeper, even without a formal education. She could crochet, cross-stitch, and sew. She made numerous baby afghans and quilts. You never had to wonder what she thought because she spoke her mind boldly. She shared her pride in her family as well as her disappointments. She encouraged and supported each person and prayed for everyone daily.

Grandmama reached up to God and out to others throughout her lifetime. She knew hardship. Growing up, her family was poor, and she remembered times when food was scarce. She kicked both colon and uterine cancer.

She knew how to fend for herself and do what needed to be done without being asked. She made a choice to walk with Christ and did not look back. She looked for ways to reach up to God for answers and then reached out to others with all she could offer, even if it weren't much. She did it for herself; she did it because her only audience was the Creator and the Savior. She lived that faith every day of her life. She taught her children, her grandchildren, and even her great-grandchildren through both words and actions.

Grandmama was present for every major milestone in the lives of her grandchildren, as much as possible. Graduations, weddings, births, and even funerals for her children's in-laws. She told all her grandchildren that their babies were really hers. She never hesitated to share an encouraging word at just the right time.

Renewal comes when we choose to live in the presence of God and trust His promises. This allows us to see others as God sees them, as valuable people in need of revival.

Moving a Piano

Moving is a big task. Whether it's across town or across the ocean or simply rearranging the furniture, moving furniture requires strength. Sherril often switches rooms around, which includes moving a large upright piano. Even with furniture sliders, it takes several strong men to move the piano. Have you ever had to move something like that? When something is too heavy for you to move, who do you call?

Sherril experienced an emotional and spiritual weight, too heavy to bear alone, in 2013. She sat alone in a doctor's office bathroom; she and her husband having just received a fatal diagnosis for their unborn son. She did the only thing left and reached out to God in her anguish. Just like an oyster creating a pearl, God began a process of creating joy from devastation. In the days that followed, Sherril faced the unknown with appreciation and renewal each day Elijah lived.

Carrying a heavy burden alone is exhausting. When you ask God to help, He lifts the burden. **This doesn't mean the pain goes away and everything goes back to normal. It does mean you learn how to stand firm, despite the pain.** God provides help through supportive friends. He gives us the opportunity to share our pain with others. Sharing the struggle often prompts healing for others. When we realize we are not alone in the fire, we experience renewal and revival.

Sherril's experience uniquely qualified her to minister to Christy in the days following the accident. She became a hedge of protection in the hospital. No one could get through the doors without her say so. At one point, there were well over a hundred people in the waiting room at one time. At times, it was overwhelming to try to love and support the crowd, pray with them, comfort them, and take all their love and grief and field it for Christy.

Cleaning up the Mess

Have you ever left a toddler alone in a room, only to come back and find diaper cream smeared on the walls or baby powder covering the room? When left alone, toddlers often make big messes. Do you ever wonder if God sees us that way? When left to our own devices, we make big messes. When we try to fix problems on our own terms, we often cause additional problems worse than the first. Perhaps that is why so often in scripture we read, "Be still" (Zechariah 2:13, Psalm 46:10-11, Exodus 14:14, Habakkuk 2:20). Strong's Concordance defines the Hebrew word raphah as a verb meaning to sink down or relax. When God tells us to be still, He's inviting us to sink down, as we would in a comfortable overstuffed chair, take a deep breath, let go of our control, and relax.

Maybe you've been greeted by a toddler mess like the one described. Did you sink into your favorite chair when you finished cleaning the mess? Did your toddler crawl up in your lap and give you hugs, kisses, and snuggles? That too, is like us. We make a big mess then we crawl into the Father's arms and ask Him to make it better and we linger awhile, thankful for His intervention. Until the next mess.

Parenthood allows us to see, on a smaller scale, how God puts up with His creation. You can be upset with your child but still love them. You attempt to convey that you know better because of your experiences. God's word also tells us over and over that He knows best. However, sometimes, renewal only happens through the mess.

Mindset of Renewal

Romans 12:2 advises us, " Do not be conformed to this world, but be transformed by the renewal of your mind, that by testing you may discern what is the will of God, what is good and acceptable and perfect."

Transformation hinges on renewing our minds. Through this renewal, we gain the ability to discern and approve what is good, pleasing to God, and aligns with His perfect will. The power of discernment allows us to recognize what aligns with goodness and God's will.

The metamorphosis of a caterpillar into a butterfly involves a complete and profound change. The caterpillar first dissolves into goop before becoming something new and beautiful. Our own transformation begins when we dissolve our old way of life and become a new creature in Christ (2 Corinthians 5:17).

To renew our minds, we should immerse ourselves in God's Word, understand its significance, and allow it to shape our thinking. The Bible isn't merely a collection of verses or a task to check off yearly; it is His communication with us and catalyst for renewal.

Pearls of Renewal

Do we understand the impact that we have when we reach out to God—whether it's for the first time for our salvation or whether it's on behalf of others in prayer or whether it's in a meal, hospitality, or kindness? God renews us as we reach out to Him and renews others through our outreach.

You may have heard or read all our stories before now. We continue to share them because with each passing year, we learn more through our grief. We continue to find value as each stage of grief brings renewal.

Stories are powerful. We continually hear from women about how impactful and helpful our stories and videos have been. In times of tragedy, it's all too easy to feel like nobody understands. We've often received message like, "I've heard Christy's story, and if she can hold on to her faith through that, I can hold on to my faith through this. I just need help." That's why we share our hearts so vulnerably, so that other women know they are not alone.

One of our speakers once talked about asking a friend to "hold her hope." She was exhausted, walking through the trenches of grief while still taking care of her family. Have you ever felt so depleted? By asking a trusted friend to hold her hope, she found renewal. She created a fire that refined her spirit and revived her soul.

God wastes nothing in His pursuit of our hearts. He bottles our tears (Psalm 56:8) and He reaches down to pull us toward Him (Psalm 18:16). In Psalm 34:18, we read, "The LORD is near to the brokenhearted and saves the crushed in spirit." The word for saves in this passage is yasha, meaning to deliver as in battle or to gain victory. God renews and revives us, giving us the victory. Often, our greatest renewal comes after our greatest trial.

Questions:

1. When you come across the word "renewal," what emotions or thoughts does it evoke for you personally? (Study Romans 12, focusing on the things that renew your mind to be more like Jesus).

2. When you reflect on the account of Shadrach, Meshach, and Abednego in the fiery furnace, how does their experience illustrate the concept of renewal amidst adversity? (Read Daniel 3:16-18. Ask yourself, Is your faith an "even if" faith?).

3. Have you ever experienced a time of renewal or transformation in your life after a significant trial or challenge? If so, how did it shape your faith and perspective? (Psalm 34:18 and Psalm 143).

4. How do you interpret the metaphor of God refining us like a precious metal in the fire, as mentioned in the chapter? How does this process relate to renewal and revival in our lives? (Psalm 66).

5. How can the renewal of our minds through God's Word lead to a deeper understanding of His will and purpose for your life? How will this keep you from conforming to the pattern of this world? (Re-read and meditate on Romans 12:2).

LOVE

One of the most overused and misused words in the English language is "love." Think about it: How many times a day do you hear or say, "I love (insert food item, TV show, song, movie, or anything else)"? Sometimes the same people who freely use the word love for inanimate objects are the ones who have the greatest difficulty expressing love in relationships.

Everyone has unique experiences that shape our ability to build relationships, communicate, and express emotions. Young children often express feelings freely, without inhibition, including love. This can sometimes be alarming to parents because as adults, we know that not all people are safe. Teaching your children safety does not have to interfere with allowing them to be loving individuals.

As we grow up, we experience rejection and begin stifling our emotions. We learn to hide our feelings to protect against pain. Even positive emotions remain unexpressed when we fear the reaction and response of others.

Above all, clothe yourselves with love, which binds us all together in perfect harmony.

Colossians 3:14 (NLT)

Defining Love

As we read the Bible, there is no doubt that love is important. Depending on your Bible version, the word love appears between 300-700 times! Let's look closer at the words used for "love" in the Bible.

In the Old Testament, we find two Hebrew words for love. In the New Testament, we find two Greek words for love. However, these are not the extent of words translated "love" in English.

The first Hebrew word is "ahab," (aw-hab') which describes a deep emotional bond, found 208 times in the Old Testament. This kind of love is about connection, whether between a husband and wife, parent and child, two best friends, or our relationship with God. This word occurs in Genesis 22 describing Abraham's love for his son Isaac and in Genesis 24 describing Jacob's love for his wife Rachel. It even occurs in the Song of Solomon when the Bride proclaims, "His banner over me is love" (2:4).

In contrast, "hesed," (kheh'-sed) is how God describes His love for us. Appearing 248 times in Scripture, this word for love is much more than a feeling. Often translated mercy or faithfulness, hesed does not depend on a deep emotional bond but faithfulness and covenant choice.

When we move to the New Testament, we learn two new words. "Agapao" or "agape" appears 142 times in the New Testament. This is considered the best description of God's love. Like "hesed" this word is more than emotions, rather it means to show honor, affection, kindness, and goodness. These actions come from integrity, whether or not that love is reciprocated. It is unconditional and often undeserved. Agape love says, "No matter what someone does to me. I choose to love them." Agape love is not based on circumstances but intentional choice.

Philia, by contrast, appears only 25 times. This is familial love or affection for someone close to you. It is not a casual acquaintance or even a general feeling for all humanity. This love takes ownership. We see this love in Romans 12:10, "Love one another with brotherly affection. Outdo one another in showing honor." It is a commitment and choice. It says, "This person is my family, and I will protect and care for them." We often use the phrase church family. We are brothers and sisters in Christ. Even in biological families, members don't always get along. However, when push comes to shove, we take care of each other. How much more should we do this in the body of Christ?

The Language of Love

From this brief word study, you can see that love connects us in our relationships—with God, with others, and with ourselves. Love establishes our identity and our mode of interaction. How do we experience this covenant connection?
Perhaps you learned the acronym JOY – Jesus, Others, Yourself. While this has some merit, it also contains some faulty thinking. The Bible says, "love the Lord your God with all your heart and with all your soul and with all your strength and with all your mind, and your neighbor as

yourself." (Luke 10:27). Did you catch that? **We cannot effectively love others unless we love ourselves.**

Allowing God's love to cover you by accepting His grace, mercy, and forgiveness for yourself, is crucial. If you don't embrace this love for yourself, you won't be able to extend it to your neighbor. The lack of self-love becomes an obstacle in relationships with neighbors, spouses, children, friends, and even within the church.

You might be asking, "But how?" or "Seriously? Self-love?" Learning to genuinely love ourselves comes from seeing ourselves as God sees us. In Psalm 139:13-14, the psalmist offers praise to the Creator. God formed us, intricately, to the tiniest detail. "I praise you, for I am fearfully and wonderfully made. Wonderful are your works; my soul knows it very well." How often do we admire God's creation in one breath and belittle ourselves in the next? Instead of putting yourself down, remember that **God calls you a trophy of grace and His bride!**

The human body contains over 37 trillion cells. Each of these cells contains your complete DNA code. Not only that, but these cells regenerate many times throughout your life. Some cells take only days, while others take years. You are fearfully and wonderfully made – not by chance or accident. God designed you uniquely and intentionally, for His purpose. We can only share God's love with others when we love ourselves as God loves us. Loving God includes learning to love yourself as His creation.

Though many of us know 1 Corinthians 13, consider that Paul's message to the church in Corinth – and to us – outlines the characteristics of love. As you look closer, you will see a contrast between what love embraces and what love resists. This passage gives us the tools we need to approach every situation in love. So often, this means stepping outside of what is comfortable, even denying our natural impulses. Love empowers us to overcome obstacles and experience life in abundance. Love transcends emotions and transforms life.

As Christians, our mandate extends beyond the comfortable. The news daily reminds us of the world's brokenness. These messages are often the loudest, leaving us mentally fatigued, spiritually drained, and crippled by fear. Yet the Gospel proclaims the antidote for fear—bold love. In 1 John 4:18, the apostle Jesus loved, wrote, "There is no fear in love, but perfect love casts out fear. For fear has to do with punishment, and whoever fears has not been perfected in love."

When we obey the Gospel, we are clothed in the love of Christ. His love drives out fear. In the first century, Christians boldly proclaimed the love of Christ, often at the cost of their lives. Our risk is so much less! It is a privilege to extend His love to others.

Begin with your inner circle – your family and closest friends. Those closest to us often get the worst of us. They see our grumpiness and grouchiness or hear our anger, bitterness, and frustrations. While there is value in venting negative feelings, those closest to us need to also see our kindness and patience. Deepen those relationships through the sharing of God's love. Offer forgiveness, expecting nothing in return. Speak the Truth in love throughout your day in every situation. As you develop this habit, you can then share with anyone you meet because everyone you meet needs God's love.

Love Languages

Dr. Gary Chapman introduced the concept of the "Five Love Languages" in 1992. Since that time over twenty million copies have been sold in 49 languages. The love languages outline five ways to understand and communicate love effectively in relationships. The five languages Chapman shares are words of affirmation, acts of service, receiving gifts, quality time, and physical touch. Some professionals discredit Chapman's idea, claiming there is no research-based evidence for these categories. Many of his critics are not following the Bible. When we look at human behavior, these categories provide a framework for how we give and receive love.

Despite the controversy of Chapman's works, the Wavemakers still find immense value in the five love languages. In fact, each of these languages can be tied into PEARLS. In all types of relationships, recognizing and respecting how each individual gives and receives love is vital in building stronger connections.

Words of affirmation include **appreciation and encouragement.** If this is your primary language, you thrive on positive words and praise.

People whose language is acts of **service** feel loved when others perform tasks that help them in some way or make their lives easier. These acts may include chores, or actions that show thoughtfulness and consideration.

For those whose language is receiving gifts, the tangible expression of love doesn't need to be extravagant. It really is the thought that counts when the gift shows intention and **appreciation**.

Quality time involves giving undivided attention, being engaged in and prioritizing time together. The time is intentional, with meaningful conversations, shared experiences, and creating new memories. Quality time **renews** relationships and offers **encouragement and appreciation**. It can even be spent **serving and praying** together!

The final love language Chapman identifies is physical touch. Perhaps easier to define than the others, physical touch is an outward show of affection that creates connection and intimacy. For many people, the outward expression is the marker of a loving relationship. When you see a couple holding hands, you can see their connectedness. Physical touch also includes caring for and assisting loved ones, even when the tasks may not be pleasurable. Such touch is a sacrificial **service**.

The Love Letter

The Word of God is comparable to love letters exchanged between two people. Imagine a scenario where one person, out of deep love, reads these letters every day, cherishing them. Even if the other person is not physically present, the love expressed in those letters sustains the connection. That is how we should spend our Bible reading time.

You might be daunted by the sheer volume of the Bible, but God is faithful. He provides His Spirit to guide us. As we faithfully devote time to the Word of God, He will continually remind us of His love. His words give guidance and connection unlike any other resource.

As you read and study the Word of God, He reveals Himself. When circumstances challenge your faith, turn to these love letters, confessing God's love for you. Repeat the truth that God loves you, no matter what, until it becomes ingrained in your beliefs. Trust that His love extends beyond your imperfections. Confess daily that you are loved by God, the Creator of the universe, and watch as His love transforms your life. Each of us cycles through forgetting and remembering God's love and faithfulness. That is why Bible study is so crucial.

The Enemy of Love

Many of us have experienced some level of rejection. Perhaps we've been abandoned, abused, manipulated, neglected, or left wondering if love is even real. So often, these acts are perpetrated by one who is supposed to love us: a parent, a significant other, a friend, or even a child. Each of these actions breaches trust and plants seeds of doubt. These painful experiences make it harder to express and receive love in healthy ways. Each of these examples is a type of trauma. Trauma of any kind changes the brain on a physical and chemical level. These changes impact the way we process information and experience emotion.

Some use the word "victim," though in recent years there's been a shift to "survivor." No matter what word you choose, the effects of trauma remain. Healing is possible and often begins with a change of mindset. In 2 Timothy 1:7, Paul reminds a young minister, "For God has not given us a spirit of fear, but of power, love, and self-control (BSB)." These are easy words to say, but difficult words to live.

Fear is one of the enemy's greatest tools. Seeds of doubt become thoughts of worthlessness. We begin to believe we are not loved or even deserving of love. The enemy plants these seeds in all human minds, beginning as early as he can gain a foothold. The longer we hold on to the pain, the longer we hold off the healing process. Consequently, the pain oozes out in our actions towards others.

Love begins with a healing process as we allow God to love and transform our mindset and perspective.
When the enemy overcomes us, we act in hurtful ways. We project our doubt, fear, and feelings of worthlessness onto those closest to us. Right now, acknowledge that such feelings are **lies**! The Bible tells us that we are loved with an everlasting love (Jeremiah 31:3), we were bought

at the cost of Christ's blood (1 Peter 1:18-19), and He knows every hair on our head (Luke 12:6-7)! You are a treasure to the Creator, worthy of His love! What the world says may hurt for a time, but it does not change your value to the Father.

The Essence of Love

Our love for God must be strong and genuine. If doubts about God's love hinder us, our ability to love Him wholeheartedly declines. God's love reaches us through firsthand experiences, relationships, divine assurance, and the written Word. Reflecting on this love enables us to navigate life's challenges with grace, mercy, and forgiveness.

In Mark 12:31, Jesus emphasizes the significance of loving your neighbor as yourself. This isn't a conditional love but a selfless, sacrificial love. It involves treating your neighbor with the same kindness, understanding, and forgiveness that you extend to yourself.

Let the love, grace, mercy, and forgiveness we've received from God guide our interactions with others. Our love for God, transforms our love for ourselves. His transformative love for us heals our hurts so that we can build healthy relationships and absolutely love our neighbor, extending the grace, mercy, and forgiveness God gives us.

Let's look closer at the nature of God. Have you ever heard someone say, "I don't believe God ever gets angry"? The wrath of God stems from His love. Just as you can be upset with your child but still love them, God's anger is rooted in His deep love for us. Even in our misguided actions, God says, "I know better; I have a better plan for you," repeatedly in His Word. When we become parents, we begin to grasp, on a small scale, the extent of God's love.

The Full Extent of Love

One of the most powerful instances illustrating God's love, other than His death and resurrection, occurs when Jesus washed His disciples' feet. In John 13, as they prepared for the feast of Passover, John records, "Jesus knew that His hour had come to leave this world and return to the Father. Having loved His own who were in the world, He loved them to the very end." Some translations use the phrase, "He now showed them the full extent of His love." In the scene that follows, Jesus takes off His outer garment and wraps a towel around His waist. He fills a basin and begins washing the feet of each disciple. This task belonged to the least of the servants in a household.

When Peter questions His actions, Jesus says, "If I do not wash you, you have no share with me." Then He asks if they understood the significance of His actions. "For I have given you an example, that you also should do just as I have done to you." Jesus shows His love with perfect humility. He didn't seek recognition or applause, but continuously reflected the essence of God's love.

In this one event, Jesus provides words of affirmation, quality time, a gift, an act of service, and physical touch. All that were present had the opportunity to receive the fullness of His love. Though Jesus does not physically do the same for us, we have the same opportunity to accept His love and share with others.

Pearls of Love

Once we grasp the depth of God's love, we gain understanding to reciprocate this love. His love encompasses physical touch, generosity of time and resources, encouraging words, and intentional interactions. Our words and actions must reflect the character of Jesus, speaking truth in love, offering with grace and mercy, and glorifying and honoring God in all our interactions.

Your love for God is intertwined with your love for others. Reiterate the truth daily: God loves you. His love empowers you to love yourself and others. Let this love be the guiding force that transforms your mind and shapes your interactions with those around you.

Choose the Word. Choose truth. Choose to believe. Choose to trust God. Choose to love.

Questions:

1. When reading about the different expressions and words for love described in the chapter (ahab, hesed, agape, philia, and love languages), what thoughts, feelings, and understanding came to your mind? In what area were you most deeply affected? Were your personal experiences and understanding of love challenged, reinforced, or shifted in any way? (Psalm 92, Hebrews 4:1-12, Proverbs 27:19).

2. How do past experiences or internalized beliefs about your own worthiness affect your understanding of love? (1 Corinthians 13).

3. The chapter discusses the importance of loving ourselves as a foundation for loving others. How do you currently view yourself in light of God's word? What steps can you take to embrace and affirm your own worthiness and value in His eyes? (Psalm 139, Matthew 10: 28-31, Luke 12:6-7, Ephesians 2:4-10, Romans 5:1-11).

4. When you reflect on the account of Jesus washing His disciples' feet, what does this act reveal about the nature of love? How can we emulate Jesus' example of humble, selfless love in our own lives and relationships? (John 13:1-20).

5. Consider the concept of the "Five Love Languages" and how understanding these languages can enhance communication and connection in relationships. Which love language(s) is most important to you, and how can you apply this understanding to create deeper connections with others? (Ephesians 4:29, Galatians 5:13, Proverbs 18:16, Ecclesiastes 4:9-10, Matthew 17:2-8).

6. Have you ever experienced a moment where you felt the full extent or even a glimpse of God's love in your life? How did that experience shape your understanding of His love, and how has it influenced the way you love others? (Psalm 36, Psalm 63, Psalm 108).

7. Which aspect of love in 1 Corinthians 13 (patience, kindness, not self-seeking, etc.) is most challenging in your daily life? How can you grow in that area of love in your interactions with others?

8. How do fear or past hurts influence your ability to give and receive love? How can you invite God's healing and transformation into those areas of your life to experience greater freedom in love? (1 Peter 2:18-25).

9. Think about a time when you witnessed or experienced an act of love that deeply impacted you. What was it about that act of love that left a lasting impression? How can you incorporate that experience into your own expressions of love towards others? (Matthew 5:13-16).

SERVICE

When you fill your life with loving God and others, service naturally follows. Like the other PEARLS, service is more natural for some than others.

The original title of this section in our videos included both serving and sharing the Word. Sherril showed many of the tools we use in our Bible study. These tools are located at the end of this book.

God desires us to serve Him by imitating the actions of Jesus during His earthly ministry. This involves performing acts of kindness and compassion without expecting acknowledgment. Serving God requires genuine commitment.

Worship is a piece of our service. However, as a song released by Acappella in 1985 says, "Worship is more than just singing a song. It's all that you say and everything that you do, it's letting His Spirit live in you."

For we are his workmanship, created in Christ Jesus for good works, which God prepared beforehand, that we should walk in them.

Ephesians 2:10

Defining Service

Unlike some of our previous word studies, six Greek and four Hebrew words translated to our English word service or servant.

One of the words, diakonía, is the root of diakonos often translated as deacon. This is an active service completed with a willing attitude and guided by faith. While this word has become associated primarily with the title of deacon, in Scripture the word applied to anyone who promoted the Word of God.

Another word, douleuó, refers to bondage or enslavement. This word also contains a willing attitude, however in this case, the attitude is one of complete submission. It is the signing over of one's rights to the power of another and giving up the right to self-govern. This word describes our nature both before and after Christ. Before Christ, we are slaves to sin (Romans 6:6, Romans 7:25). After our baptism, we are slaves to Christ (Romans 6:22, 1 Corinthians 7:22). Paul the apostle introduces himself in his letter to the Romans as a "slave to Christ" (Romans 1:1).

Our English definitions of service are equally diverse. Service can be doing something for someone, a period of employment, a formal assembly, routine maintenance, or supplying utilities. When we view service instead through the eyes of Scripture, we know that service requires both a willing Spirit and surrender to God. In terms of utilities, we often surrender payment, without willingness – or our willingness goes only as far as what we need at the time.

Worship includes both vertical and horizontal components, like all the words that comprise PEARLS. Vertically, worship is praise and adoration to the Father. Horizontally worship edifies the congregation. It's called a worship service or an assembly. This is not by coincidence. Have you ever heard someone say, "I didn't get much from church today."? Maybe you've even said this yourself. Consider that your purpose is not to receive, but to give. As your focus changes, you will experience edification.

One thing the origins of service have in common is work. Érgon, the Greek word for work is an action that completes an inner desire. This implies both intention and purpose. As Christians, our work is to be about the Father's business. James 1:27 says, "Religion that is pure and undefiled before God the Father is this: to visit orphans and widows in their affliction, and to keep oneself unstained from the world." In Matthew 25:34-46, Jesus gives His disciples a glimpse into Judgment. Our focus will be the first half, when the King addresses the sheep to His right.

> "Come, you who are blessed by my Father, inherit the kingdom prepared for you from the foundation of the world. For I was hungry and you gave me food, I was thirsty and you gave me drink, I was a stranger and you welcomed me, I was naked and you clothed me, I was sick and you visited me, I was in prison and you came to me." Then the righteous will answer him, saying, "Lord, when did we see you hungry and

feed you, or thirsty and give you drink? And when did we see you a stranger and welcome you, or naked and clothe you? And when did we see you sick or in prison and visit you?" And the King will answer them, "Truly, I say to you, as you did it to one of the least of these my brothers, you did it to me."

Qualifications of Service

Our service to God includes everything we do to serve others. When you feel unqualified, remember that when you accepted the Gospel, God qualified you for His calling! (Romans 8). He gave you His Spirit that you may produce fruit (Galatians 5:25). To produce fruit, you must be active.

Before you argue, consider the assortment of God's tools in the Bible. In the book of Judges alone, we see Ehud's dagger (3:16), Shamgar's oxgoad (3:31) Jael's hammer (4:21), Gideon's horns and torches (7:16), a woman's millstone (9:53), and Samson uses the jawbone of donkey (15:15). God's deliverances are often as unique as the people He chooses. Consider Exodus 4:2. God asks Moses, "What's in your hand?" and proceeds to use a staff to carry out mighty works.

If you think you have nothing to offer, put the tools in your hand into the hand of God. Just as in the cases of Shamgar's oxgoad, Moses' rod, David's sling (1 Samuel 17), the widow's meal and oil (1 Kings 17:7-16), Dorcas' needle and thread (Acts 9:36-42), or the simple lunch of a little boy (John 6:8-11), when we surrender what's in our hand and submit to His word, God does great things.

Ages and Stages

Max Lucado said, "No one can do everything, but everyone can do something." Children can serve, stay at home moms can serve, empty nesters can serve, widows can serve. Did you know that the Hebrew language has no word for retirement? As Christians, our retirement plan is Heaven. We get to work for the Kingdom, as long as life allows!

In every stage of life, God has prepared works for you (Ephesians 2:10). When you are home with babies and toddlers, your service looks different than when you have school-age children and teenagers. When you are single, your opportunities are different than when you have a family and home of your own. When children leave home or you retire from your chosen career, yet another new set of opportunities arises!

God knows our limitations, whether physical, emotional, mental, or spiritual, and His plans for us include all of it! Consider that we are not powerful enough to mess up His purpose. He gives us all we need (2 Peter 1:3). God's grace is sufficient, even in our weakness (2 Corinthians 12:9). Our service is an act of surrender, allowing us to work through our challenges while fulfilling His purpose.

Personality Types

Personality types fall into two broad categories: introversion and extroversion. It is important to note that these personality types are not solely dictated by social interactions. In many ways, these categories are defined by how individuals recharge their energy.

The Bible contains wisdom, even in the context of human nature and behavior. When we use the guidance on understanding provided in Scripture, we gain much more insight into ourselves and others than we do by observation, personality tests or textbooks.

Throughout Scripture we read of the importance of solace and solitude. Psalm 46:10 says, "Be still, and know that I am God." This stillness is not idleness, but quiet reflection in the presence of God. We find peace only when we spend time with God. This is worship.

Jesus frequently withdrew to solitary places to pray and recharge, but He also was often the center of a crowd. If the Son of God needed to take the time to recharge, we ought to do the same.

In Corinthians 12:18-20, the apostle Paul compares members of the body of Christ, the church, to the various parts of the human body. This metaphor highlights the idea that everyone possesses unique strengths which contribute to the functioning of the whole community.

Personality is more of a spectrum than set categories. Many people have both introverted and extroverted traits. When you understand your own personality, your service to God and others will benefit.

Everyone has a Ministry.

Before His ascension, Jesus told the disciples to "Go into all the world and preach the gospel" (Matthew 28:19, Mark 16:15). When you study the word "go" in the Greek, it does not merely mean travel from one place to another. This word implies that as they were on the journey, at every opportunity, they were to preach the Good News. The same thought is expressed in Deuteronomy 6:7, "And you shall teach them diligently to your children and speak of them when you sit at home and when you walk along the road, when you lie down and when you get up." Whatever act of service you choose, whatever your stage of life, "as you are going," you get to share God's message!

Throughout the endless tasks of motherhood, the complexities of marriage, work demands, household chores, and the ongoing struggle to balance our spiritual, physical, mental, and emotional well-being we find our unique gifts of service. Again, the Wavemakers do not teach from a pedestal. We do not have it all figured out. We are walking the same path, and as we go, we share what we have learned. Our experiences may not mirror yours exactly, but we're committed to sharing. Even when the experiences and raw emotions are ugly, part of helping others is going through the darkness together.

Angie and her husband had a friend in college that said, "If you aren't the missionary, then you are the mission field." It's been over twenty years since that conversation and the words continue to make an impact. More recently, while stationed in Germany, Angie met with a group of women. The question came up, "How do I serve when I'm busy caring for my babies, even during church services?" The young mom was visibly upset that she couldn't devote more time to Bible study and ministry. An older woman looked at this anxious mom full of love and grace. She said, "Right now, your children are your talents. Invest in them."

As women, our first place of service is in our home. We instruct our children daily, as we go. In the beginning, it may be mostly "no" or "don't." As your children grow, the days are filled with "can I tell you something?" and "why?" Each conversation is an act of service.

Mamas, we know you are often tired, impatient, and overwhelmed. Take the time to answer them while they are little, so the conversations continue when it matters. Caring for our children aligns with God's plan. We are to train them in the ways of the Lord (Ephesians 6:4, Proverbs 22:6). God doesn't expect more than we're capable of in our current season. Our talents are unique to the tasks God wants us to do.

Outside of our homes, we serve each other in our local congregation and community. This can be providing a meal, giving someone a ride, or helping with a specific need. Christy often shares with new homeschoolers a lesson she learned from Sherril. Sometimes schoolwork is not the most important thing to do. Some days, the best education you can give your child is teaching them to serve with you. Even littles can help take a meal to someone or make cards.

What if you work in an office? You can serve in simple ways. Write an encouraging quote on the whiteboard in the break room or leave anonymous notes for your co-workers. If you know your co-workers well, you could even surprise them with small gifts, something as simple and subtle as leaving someone a package of their favorite candy.

At some point, it may even involve recognizing that someone is going through a tough time and offering a kind word like, "I want you to know I'm thinking about you, I'm praying for you, I'm here if you need anything." Whether they confide in you or not, you have opened a door. Service is not about imposing ourselves on others. God already knows their needs. Instead, it's about creating opportunities for connection and kindness.

In early 2019, Christy found a network marketing trainer named Ray Higdon. He initiated "Wealth Wednesday." Every week, he encourages his audience to "do a random act of kindness for a stranger that involves a financial exchange." This may include paying for the person behind you in the drive-thru, tipping extra at a restaurant, or putting money in a diaper box. You are only limited by your imagination. After the accident, we renamed Wealth Wednesday to Wavemaker Wednesday. We extended the definition to include acts of service toward anyone, including people you know. Wavemakers are people determined to make a difference in the world, one act, one person, at a time. This may include taking a meal to a new mom or someone recovering from surgery, taking care of someone's yard, or simply sitting with someone who is hurting. **Small ripples turn into big waves.**

Pearls of Service

Service encompasses all the other letters in PEARLS. We serve those on our prayer list. Our acts of service offer encouragement, show appreciation, renew spirits, and express love.

We are servants of the Most High God, and we have a responsibility to share Him with others. One of our past speakers talked about how amazing it is that God allows us to touch His Word and His work. What a blessing! As the Wavemakers continue, we want you to know that we do not approach you from the place of arrival, but from the middle of the journey. Our deepest desire is to serve you through the thick of it.

At the end of each day, spend a few minutes reflecting. What went well? What needs improvement? What was the best part of the day? What did you learn? As you reflect, express gratitude that God allows you to be part of His work! You are one thread in His tapestry. In your daily acts of service, whatever your stage of life, you can make waves!

Serve where you are. Share in God's work. Whether through small gestures or profound conversations, **every act of service plays a part in God's grand plan.** God equipped us for service, using our unique talents, and called us to share His message.

Questions:

1. How does serving others reflect our devotion to God? (Study Matthew 25 focusing on the service and devotion).

2. When we grasp the truth that God has chosen, qualified, empowered, and equipped us for specific tasks and roles within His kingdom because of His infinite wisdom and grace, it gives us confidence and assurance. How does that allow you to see your identity in Christ? How has He uniquely qualified you for service? (Reflect on Ephesians 2:1-10 and Romans 8).

3. How can we find strength in knowing that He equips us for His work, when faced with feelings of inadequacy? (Read and reflect on Philippians 4:10-13).

4. In what ways can different stages of life provide unique opportunities for service? (Ecclesiastes 3:1-13).

5, How does your understanding of service deepen when you explore the various Greek and Hebrew words translated as "service" or "servant" in Scripture, such as diakonía and douleuó? How does this understanding influence your approach to serving others even during challenges? (Meditate on Colossians 3:22-24).

4. How can you use your unique strengths and abilities to contribute to the functioning of the body and further God's kingdom? (Study God's design and desire for the body to function according to the analogy of the body of Christ in 1 Corinthians 12:18-31).

5. Psalm 46:10 encourages us to "Be still and know that I am God." How do you prioritize quiet reflection and communion with God in your life? How does this practice of solitude and worship replenish your energy and equip you for service?

6. Reflecting on the story of Moses and his staff in Exodus 4:2, think about the "tools" or resources God has placed in your hands for service. How can you surrender these resources to God and allow Him to work through you to accomplish great things?

7. In what ways do different stages of life present unique opportunities for service? How can you embrace your current stage of life as a platform for serving God and others right now, regardless of challenges or limitations? (Study these women who served at different stages in different ways Mary in Luke 1:26-38, Esther in Esther 1-4, Naomi in Ruth 1, and Deborah in Judges 4-5).

8. Considering the concept of "Wavemaker Wednesday" and the practice of performing random acts of kindness, how can you incorporate intentional acts of service into your daily routine? How might these small gestures create ripple effects of positivity and impact in your community? (Memorize Luke 6:38).

9. Reflecting on your own personality type, how does understanding your strengths and preferences shape your approach to service? How can you tailor your acts of service to align with your personality while still stretching beyond your comfort zone? (Study Exodus 3-4 contemplating Moses being stretched beyond his comfort zone).

10. Reflecting on your daily experiences of service, take a moment to express gratitude for the opportunity to participate in God's work. Now make a list of opportunities you passed up and look for those opportunities to come around again and how you can be ready to serve the next time. (Read James 4:13-17 and Ephesians 4:25-32).

BECOMING PEARLS

When we put these letters together, we have a beautiful strand of pearls. Beautiful things emerge from the crucible of challenging circumstances: diamonds, born from unimaginable pressure; amethysts, forged amidst incredible heat; and pearls, formed through profound pain. In each instance, adversity gives rise to rare and exquisite treasures, testament to the transformative power of struggle.

The more time we spend in prayer, the more we encourage and appreciate. This leads to a renewal that allows us to love as God loves and serve selflessly. As we grow in our relationship with God, He gives us more opportunities to grow in our relationships with others. God desires that we conform to the image of His Son. God's purpose from the beginning was that all people would seek Him and then lead others to salvation as well.

We would be remiss if we failed at sharing the hope we have with you. If you were to search the internet for "the plan of salvation," you would see over sixty-five million articles. Many of these present a false Gospel that ends with a prayer asking Jesus into your heart. You will find no such prayer or example in Scripture.

The next thing you will notice in several of the articles is a focus on earthly happiness. One religion even calls the plan of salvation "the great plan of happiness" with the focus being earthly contentment. This is also contrary to the Scriptures.

An estimated four thousand religions exist worldwide. These tend to fall into one of the following five groups: Christianity, Islam, Buddhism, Hinduism, and Judaism. Globally, forty-five thousand denominations claim Christianity. In John 14:6, Jesus tells His disciples, "I am the way, and the truth, and the life. No one comes to the Father except through me." Jesus also warns them in Matthew 7:13-14, saying "Enter by the narrow gate. For the gate is wide and the way is easy that leads to destruction, and those who enter by it are many. For the gate is narrow and the way is hard that leads to life, and those who find it are few." He goes on to warn them of false teachers and how to recognize them. Jesus concludes in Matthew 7:21-23, "Not everyone who says to me, 'Lord, Lord,' will enter the kingdom of heaven, but the one who does the will of my Father who is in heaven. On that day many will say to me, 'Lord, Lord, did we not prophesy in your name, and cast out demons in your name, and do many mighty works in your name?' And then will I declare to them, 'I never knew you; depart from me, you workers of lawlessness.'"

God is not the author of confusion (1 Corinthians 14:33). He is firmly against any teaching that is in opposition to Him. We must turn to the Word of God to determine what we must do to be saved. We invite you to examine the Scriptures with us and test yourself (2 Corinthians 13:5). Salvation is pass/fail; one is either saved or not.

In 1 John 5:13, the apostle says, "I write these things to you who believe in the name of the Son of God, that you may know that you have eternal life." If the inspired apostle said we may know, then the way to salvation is not a mystery! The word "know" in the Greek, eídō, conveys much more than knowledge. Instead, eídō bridges the gap between our physical sight and our mental or spiritual comprehension. That raises the question, **how do we know we are saved?**

During the Restoration Movement in the 1800s, Walter Scott introduced a framework consisting of six points, outlining that man provides faith, repentance, and baptism, while God provides remission of sins, the gift of the Holy Spirit, and eternal life. However, it is noted that belief, repentance, and confession are not considered as "steps." These are a daily practice for the Christian.

In Mark 16:15-16, the order presented by Jesus includes hearing, believing, and baptism **prior** to being saved. Wes McAdams wrote, "My baptism was not me reaching the top of a staircase; it was me – in response to the Good News – desperately throwing myself at the feet of a gracious God, appealing to Him for salvation and a good conscience." It wasn't until the Protestant Reformation in the 1600s that people argued that salvation occurs at the moment of faith and that baptism is unrelated to salvation, equating it to a work.

The only way we receive salvation is that we first hear the Good News (Romans 10:10-17). We have hope because someone taught us the gospel. Maybe you grew up in a Christian home, as Angie and Christy did. Your parents taught you and encouraged you to study the Bible. Maybe you grew up like Sherril, knowing about God, even reading the Bible, but not understanding the message of hope.

When we confess (agree with God that sin is sin) and repent (turn away from and go in the opposite direction), we submit to God's authority. To wash our sins away, we die to ourselves through baptism. Baptism is the ultimate act of submission, not a work. We cannot immerse ourselves. At baptism, one enters Christ for forgiveness, marking the start of a new life. We will still face temptation and fall short, but we have the Spirit of God to keep us on the right path and continually forgive us. (Romans 6).

Let's talk about this word baptism. The English word is a transliteration of the Greek "baptizo," meaning to immerse or submerge underwater. Historically, this is the same word used for the sinking of a ship. Metaphorically, this word means to be overwhelmed, as in the case of debt. Throughout ancient history, immersion was both a literal and figurative cleansing. Water washes away impurities from the skin. The submissive action allows us to break free from sin and become a new creature in Christ (Galatians 3:27, Colossians 2:12, 1 Peter 3:21).

Every conversion to Christianity in the book of Acts includes baptism. Not once did the person ask, "Do I have to do that?" They simply obeyed. Even Paul, who met Jesus on the Road to Damascus and repented, still had to be immersed to receive forgiveness and the Holy Spirit. The book of Acts contains only one example of the Holy Spirit being given before baptism, in the instance of Cornelius, the centurion and his household. This occurred to show the Jewish Christians that there was no longer a distinction between Jew and Gentile: salvation was available to all people. Even though they received the Spirit, they still had to be baptized to receive forgiveness and be added to the Kingdom.

When studying the Scriptures, we must remember that chapter and verse divisions are manmade. When the Roman church first received Paul's letter, they listened to its reading in entirety. Chapter divisions would not be added until 1227 by Stephen Langton. The adding of verse divisions happened much later. A Jewish rabbi named Nathan, divided the Old Testament in 1448. In 1551, Rober Estienne (aka Stephanus) introduced verse divisions in the New Testament. **Context matters.**

When you study the Bible, put away your preconceived ideas. Consider the historical context. Who was the original audience? What was the purpose of the writing at the time? What was going on during that time in history? Next, remember that God's Word is unchanging (Isaiah 40:8, Malachi 3:6, Matthew 24:35).

If you find that you are not in compliance with the Bible, whether in terms of salvation or another area of walking in agreement with God, the Good News is that you have Hope! You can change directions and make your life right with God. No matter how old you are, it is never too late to obey the Gospel. If you sincerely desire to serve the Lord, then He is faithful. **When you seek the Lord with your whole heart, He guides you to the way of eternal life.**

Questions:

1. Where did the scriptures come from and what is the purpose of the scriptures? (Paul tells Timothy all the scriptures are breathed by God for teaching, reproof, correction, and for training in righteousness in 2 Timothy 3:15-17).

2. How do we know Jesus is who He says He is? (Jesus Himself tells us that He is the Testimony of God, and that God, through the scriptures, is His Witness so we can believe Him in John 5:19-47. Reading through the Bible from beginning to end and studying it, there is no doubt that Jesus is the Savior).

3. Why did Jesus come to Earth? (John tells us Jesus is the Word of God and came to the Earth in the flesh and lived among us to take away the sins of the world, and John, God, and the Spirit witnessed it in John 1:1-34).

4. How does God speak to us today? (In Hebrews 1:1, the writer tells us how God has spoken to His people in the past and how He speaks to people today).

5. How does God sanctify His people today? (Jesus prayed that the Father would sanctify [make holy or purify] those who believed in Him and that the Word is true and will sanctify us. Read John 17, focusing on verse 17).

6. Before Jesus' death, how were people forgiven of sin under the law of Moses? (Faith in God's law or the sacrifices for sin? Read Leviticus 4:1-31).\

7. Why do we trust the apostles and what they taught in the book of Acts? (Matthew 16:13-20).

8. After Jesus' death, burial, and resurrection, how were sins forgiven? (Remember Jesus' crucifixion is the one sacrifice for all, 1 Peter 3:18. Read how sins were forgiven after His resurrection throughout the book of Acts 2:14-47; 8:4-25, 26-40; 9:1-19; 10; 16:11-15, 25-34, 19:1-10 – Even better, read the entire book of Acts from beginning to end, also Romans 6, Colossians 2:8-15, 1 Peter 3:18-22).

APPENDIX: RESOURCES AND TOOLS

YouVersion Bible Application available on IOS and Android
Biblehub.com (or Application available on IOS and Android)
BibleAtlas.org

All PEARLS video content:
https://wavemakerslife.com/pearlsvideos

https://5lovelanguages.com/

We enjoy conversations, studying the Word, and sharing in the lives of others. If you would like to continue any conversation or study from this book, feel free to contact us!

HOW TO FIND US:

Wavemaker Website: https://www.wavemakerslife.com/

Facebook Group:
https://www.facebook.com/groups/wavemakerlife

Facebook Bible reading group:
https://www.facebook.com/groups/wavemakerbiblestudy

YouTube link:
https://www.youtube.com/c/WavemakerLifeHopeMinistry

E-Mail: wavemakerministry@gmail.com

Made in the USA
Middletown, DE
03 June 2024